ELT Development Series

SERIES EDITOR Thomas S. C. Farrell

Project-Based Learning

Erin Knoche Laverick

tesol press

www.tesol.org/bookstore

TESOL International Association
1925 Ballenger Avenue
Alexandria, Virginia, 22314 USA
www.tesol.org

Director of Publishing and Product Development: Myrna Jacobs
Copy Editor: Sarah J. Duffy
Cover: Citrine Sky Design
Interior Design & Layout: Capitol Communications, LLC
Printing: Gasch Printing, LLC

ISBN 978-1-945351-31-0
Library of Congress Control No. 2018952189

Table of Contents

Series Editor's Preface

The English Language Teacher Development (ELTD) Series consists of a set of short resource books for ESL/EFL teachers that are written in a jargon free and accessible manner for all types of teachers of English (native, non-native, experienced and novice teachers). The ELTD series is designed to offer teachers a theory-to-practice approach to second language teaching and each book offers a wide variety range of practical teaching approaches and methods of the topic at hand. Each book also offers time for reflections for each teacher to interact with the materials presented in the book. The books can be used in pre-service settings or in in-service courses and can also be used by individual looking for ways to refresh their practice.

Erin Laverick's book, *Project Based Learning* (PBL) outlines and discusses how teachers can design, implement, oversee, and assess PBL in their classrooms. Laverick explains what PBL is (and how it contrasts it with Task Based Language Teaching (TBLT)). After defining PBL, the book discusses the benefits of using PBL, how to implement it, how to plan PBL lessons as well as how to conduct assessment related to PBL lessons. In addition, the final chapter offers teachers a means of avoiding particular challenges with implementing PBL with remedies presented. *Project Based Learning* is another valuable addition to the literature in our profession and to the ELTD series.

I am very grateful to the authors who contributed to the ELTD Series for sharing their knowledge and expertise with other TESOL professionals. It is truly an honor for me to work with each of these authors as they selflessly gave up their valuable time for the advancement of TESOL.

Thomas S.C. Farrell

CHAPTER 1

Introduction

This book introduces project-based learning (PBL) and explains how it can be effectively implemented into classes with English language learners (ELLs). The primary goal of the book is to offer teachers an overview of PBL so they may begin to design, implement, oversee, and formatively and summatively assess PBL in their classrooms.

The book comprises six chapters. Chapter 2 defines PBL and compares and contrasts it with task-based learning (TBL). The benefits of using PBL with ELLs are also explained. Chapter 3 introduces classroom implementation of PBL and explains strategies for using a process approach to complete projects, similar to the writing process. As part of the process approach, design and use of mini lessons are also discussed. Chapter 4 presents how to use mini lessons to scaffold to a final product, including lesson planning and implementation. Chapter 5 explains formative and summative assessment, including rubric design, and discusses reflection as a means of assessment. Finally, Chapter 6 explores some challenges that may be encountered when implementing PBL and presents remedies.

After reading this book, instructors should be able to design, implement, oversee, and assess a project with ease and confidence.

CHAPTER 2

Project-Based Learning

This chapter defines PBL and connects it to the communicative approach. It discusses the benefits of using PBL in an English language classroom and compares and contrasts PBL with task-based learning (TBL). A unit plan for a beginning-level communication skills class is provided to demonstrate how PBL and TBL are similar and different.

By the end of this chapter, you will be able to answer the following questions:

- What is PBL?
- How does PBL align with the principles of communicative language teaching?
- What are the benefits of using PBL in an English language classroom?
- How is PBL similar to and different from TBL?

As indicated by the name, project-based learning involves students refining and honing their language skills through the completion of projects both in and outside of the classroom. It requires teachers to create a classroom culture of creativity and engagement in which students share their work and reflect on the processes they use to create and complete their projects (Cooper & Murphy, 2016). It moves away from a teacher-centered style of teaching where students sit passively in a class and are rarely given the opportunity to put their ideas into action or practice their language skills in authentic environments. Instead, PBL engages students through the act of inquiry (Leat, 2017) and promotes the development of critical thinking skills.

Specifically, in the field of English language instruction, PBL is a means for students to improve their language and critical thinking skills in tandem. Tricia Hedge (1993) first introduced PBL as a means for English language learners (ELLs) to develop their communicative competence and fluency. She defined PBL as follows:

> A project is an extended task which usually integrates language skills through a number of activities. These activities combine in working towards an agreed goal and may include planning, the gathering of information through reading, listening, interviewing, etc., discussion of the information, problem solving, oral or written reporting, and display. (Hedge, 1993, p. 276)

While PBL is used with many types of learners and in many types of classrooms, for English language classes it includes the integration of language skills to complete these extended tasks. Hedge (1993) noted additional specifications for PBL use in an ELL classroom, including using authentic materials, creating a student-centered classroom, sequencing tasks to scaffold the final project, and students accepting responsibility in completing the project both in and outside of the classroom.

Communicative Language Teaching and PBL

Because PBL calls for the integration of language skills as a means for students to increase their fluency, it aligns well with the communicative language teaching (CLT) approach. The CLT approach has been commonly used in English language classrooms since the 1970s for many types of learners—children, adults, postsecondary students, and so on. Brown and Lee (2015) have outlined seven characteristics of the communicative approach. The characteristics of CLT are helpful in understanding how PBL enhances English language learning and how it can be implemented into a classroom where CLT is applied.

- CLT focuses on all aspects of language (integration of skills).
- CLT focuses on the function of language, with form being secondary.
- CLT focuses on fluency first and then accuracy.
- CLT focuses on real-world contexts.
- CLT focuses on students using language outside of the classroom.
- CLT focuses on the teacher as a facilitator or guide.
- CLT focuses on student-centered learning.

As previously indicated, like CLT, PBL calls for the integration of language skills so that all aspects of language are taught. Projects often focus on real-life contexts and are collaborative, requiring students to negotiate for meaning with their instructors, their peers, and even outside participants, depending on the assignment. In PBL, the teacher creates a student-centered learning environment and facilitates or guides students through the completion of their projects.

For example, a teacher assigns students to read a passage from a textbook and answer comprehension questions. The students read and complete their assignment, but the teacher notices the students are disengaged and simply going through the motions of completing the assignment. They do not interact with their peers, and outside of the class they do not discuss what they have read. The teacher decides to better engage students through their assignments and assigns a novel for the class to read and discuss both in and outside of the classroom. After reading the novel, the teacher places students into groups and assigns each group to design a movie trailer about the novel. The creation of the movie trailer, like the completion of the comprehension questions, demonstrates students' comprehension of the novel. However, the project requires them to engage in a more thoughtful inquiry of the novel through discussing and analyzing the text with their peers in order to design the movie trailers.

If we look at Bloom's revised taxonomy, as developed by Anderson and Krathwohl (2001), we see that when students read a text and answer comprehension questions, they only demonstrate their ability to remember and understand the reading assignment. Both of these outcomes fall in the lower end of the taxonomy pyramid. However, through the creation of the movie trailer, students not only demonstrate the ability to remember and understand the novel, they also apply what they learned from the novel by analyzing and evaluating the text in order to determine what information should be included in the movie trailers. Indeed, the movie trailer project demonstrates students' ability to comprehend the novel and encourages them to develop their higher order language and thinking skills. These outcomes appear in the highest point of the taxonomy pyramid. At the end of the project, students share their work with each other and reflect on the process they used to complete the final project and the overall product.

REFLECTIVE QUESTIONS

- Have you ever designed or used a project such as a movie trailer?

- How did you engage with your students throughout the project?

- How did your students use their language skills to create the project?

If you have designed an assignment such as the movie trailer example, then you have used PBL in your classroom. For an assignment to be considered PBL, it should

- require students to create an original or authentic product;
- encourage students to think critically;
- be made public and shared with peers, family, community members, and so on;
- encourage collaboration through completion of the project;
- encourage students to reflect during and after completion of the project.

REFLECTIVE QUESTION

- How does the movie trailer project meet the five criteria listed above for PBL?

Indeed, the movie trailer assignment is an excellent example of PBL, as it required students to create an original text and think critically. Students had to make inferences and analyze the novel in order to create their trailers. The process they used to complete the project was collaborative, as they worked in groups to design the trailers. Students' work was made public or shared with an outside audience. And finally, after students shared their work, they reflected in their groups about the process they used to complete the trailer and the outcomes of their final projects.

In addition to the movie trailer, here are some other projects:

- creating a diorama to demonstrate comprehension of the characters, setting, and main conflict of a novel or short story

- writing a script and performing a play with peers

- researching a topic and creating a podcast to present the research findings to an audience

- writing a recipe and then demonstrating how to prepare the dish

- conducting an interview and creating a multimodal composition to share the findings with an audience

REFLECTIVE QUESTION

- Can you think of other possible projects that would work well in your classroom?

The Benefits of Using PBL

There are multiple benefits to using PBL in an English language classroom. To begin, projects encourage students to further negotiate for meaning and use English in authentic and meaningful contexts. Indeed, second language acquisition theory has proven that group work is beneficial for students in learning English. Lessard-Clouston (2016), in exploring Long's interactionist model, has written that such interaction increases students' input and output of the language. In addition, Ellis (2003) has written that group work "increases language practice opportunities, it improves the quality of student talk, it helps to individualize instruction, it promotes a positive affective climate, and it motivates students to learn" (p. 598). In other words, group work reduces teacher talk time and creates an environment where students practice using the language. In addition, Long and Porter (1985) have written that group work offers students strategies for using the language that they can employ outside of the classroom as well, because their speech is not staged or forced. Therefore, collaboration in PBL allows students to go beyond practicing the language, increasing their abilities to use English outside of the classroom in authentic settings.

In addition to group work, PBL offers students choices in their class work. Beckett (2002, p. 54) wrote that PBL is "exploratory in nature" and that outcomes of the projects vary, depending on students' work ethic and the individual choices they make while creating projects. Therefore, PBL requires students to take further ownership of their work more so than worksheets or other tasks assigned in textbooks.

Finally, Campbell (2012) noted that PBL allows for differentiated instruction. While students workshop their projects, instructors have time to better address individual students' needs and offer them feedback. Feedback is further addressed in Chapter 5, which discusses the assessment of projects.

REFLECTIVE QUESTION

- What are some other benefits of using PBL in your classroom?

How Is PBL Similar and/or Different From TBL?

PBL is often confused with TBL. According to Bygate, Skehan, and Swain (2001), "A task is an activity which requires learners to use language, with emphasis on meaning, to obtain an objective" (p. 11). Bygate et al. focus on one activity in their definition. Yet PBL requires students to engage in several tasks in order to complete a project.

For example, a teacher assigns students to read and discuss a short story. After reading and discussing the text, students design a diorama that presents the setting, characters, and conflict of the story. After reading and note taking, students visually arrange the dioramas to ensure they include all the key components from the novel (setting, characters, plot, etc.). They then prepare a presentation and share their work with the class and the teacher. The teacher facilitates the development and arrangement of the presentations so students are best prepared to share their work. After presenting their work, students reflect on the process of creating the dioramas and their final projects. This entire process takes several weeks to complete.

The teacher, in lesson planning for the project, may design smaller tasks or mini lessons for students to complete throughout the unit; for example, she or he may design a lesson on how to take notes. The students may complete this task in class to practice taking notes while reading. Tasks, especially those completed during a class period, serve as stand-alone activities. Therefore, these task-based lessons are only one piece of the entire unit or project, with the goal of ensuring students are on track to complete the project. In other words, the tasks scaffold to the completion of the project.

Table 1 demonstrates the differences between planning for day-to-day lessons (TBL) and planning for a project for a beginning-level communication skills course for adult learners (PBL). In these lessons, students learn to write and talk about recipes using proper measurements.

As indicated in Table 1, the instructor that used TBL spent only 3 days on instruction and 1 day on assessment. The activities allowed for individualized instruction, practice, and formative assessment, and students met each objective; however, students were not given the opportunity to extend their language learning and further their abilities to collaborate, critically think, share their recipes with an audience, or reflect on what they learned. Therefore, if we return to Anderson and Krathwohl's (2001) revised Bloom's taxonomy, we see how the PBL unit, in contrast, extended students' learning and helped them acquire higher level thinking and language skills.

Also, as noted in Table 1, the project allowed time for students to workshop and confer with their instructor. Workshop days allow the instructor to provide students with further individualized instruction on content they may struggle to comprehend or language that is difficult to use. For example, a student may struggle with writing his or her biography for the cookbook. The instructor can use the workshop times to assist the student in writing a biography by modeling or using sentence forms to help the student write a draft. Then on the next workshop day, the student can bring his or her draft to the instructor for further feedback. This scaffolding creates opportunity for the sort of individualized instruction that is so important for ELLs as they acquire the language.

Table 1. Example of Task-Based Versus Project-Based Planning

	Task-Based Planning	Project-Based Planning
Day 1	**Objective:** Students will be able to identify measurements in recipes. ● The instructor introduces measurements, providing students with a handout or some other visual aid. ● Students complete a worksheet or a manipulative in which they match the correct measurement with its abbreviation (e.g., tsp. = teaspoon). ● The instructor goes over the activity and may assign homework such as a worksheet before students leave for the day.	**Objective:** Students will be able to identify measurements in recipes. ● The instructor introduces a project in which students will write a recipe, prepare the dish for their classmates, and collaboratively create a cookbook. ● After reviewing the assignment sheet and rubric, the instructor introduces measurements and has students complete a manipulative to match the correct measurements. ● For homework, students brainstorm their favorite recipes.
Day 2	**Objective:** Students will be able to use vocabulary that is common when cooking and reading recipes. ● The instructor may use PowerPoint or the Internet to display target vocabulary. ● Students may write sentences using the key vocabulary.	**Objective:** Students will be able to use vocabulary that is common when cooking and/or reading recipes. ● The instructor may use PowerPoint or the Internet to display target vocabulary and model how to write a recipe using measurements and key ingredients. ● Using the brainstorming they created on Day 1, students narrow their focus, select one recipe, and begin drafting the recipe in proper format.
Day 3	**Objective:** Students will be able to identify measurements in recipes and use vocabulary that is commonly found in recipes. ● The instructor may review lessons from Days 1 and 2 and have students complete an in-class activity as an informal assessment.	**Objective:** Students will be able to identify and use measurements in recipes as well as use vocabulary that is commonly found in recipes. ● Students continue writing their recipes. ● The instructor serves as a facilitator and asks questions as students continue to write their recipes.

continued on next page

Table 1. *(continued)*

	Task-Based Planning	Project-Based Planning
Day 4	Students may be quizzed on materials.	**Objective:** Students will be able to talk about their recipes and explain the process for making the dish. ● Students bring their written recipes to class. ● The instructor shows a cooking demonstration or models how to talk about food. ● Students begin to rehearse their presentations.
Day 5		● Students continue to rehearse their presentations.
Day 6		● In front of the class, students demonstrate how to make the dish using props.
Day 7		● Continue presentations if needed.
Day 8		**Objective:** Students will be able to create a class cookbook in which they include their names, biographies, written recipes, and any eye-catching visuals for the audience. ● Workshop day. The instructor acts as a facilitator and assists students as they work together on the cookbook.
Day 9		● Workshop day
Day 10		● Workshop day
Day 11		**Objective:** Students will reflect on the project, discussing their overall contributions to the cookbook, how they would improve if they had more time to work, and the value of creating the cookbook. ● Final class cookbook is due.

Conclusion

This chapter introduced PBL and explained how it can be used when applying the communicative approach in an English language classroom. It also discussed benefits such as increasing students' critical thinking skills, improving their abilities to negotiate for meaning, and enhancing their opportunities to use English in authentic settings. Finally, PBL was compared and contrasted with TBL. The next chapter discusses best practices, specifically for using a process approach, when implementing PBL in the classroom.

CHAPTER 3

Implementing PBL

This chapter introduces best practices for implementing PBL in a classroom for ELLs, including using workshop time and instructor conferences to differentiate instruction. The chapter also explains best practices for using a process approach so that students can effectively complete their projects.

By the end of this chapter, you will be able to answer the following questions:

- What are some effective strategies for implementing PBL in the classroom?
- How is PBL similar to the writing process?

As previously noted, implementing PBL requires the instructor to set goals for the long term rather than planning segmented daily lesson plans that focus on smaller tasks. That is, projects require an instructor to plan several weeks ahead. Yet, depending on how students complete their projects, mini lessons may still be needed to meet individual students' needs. Therefore, flexibility is important.

For example, if a teacher assigns a project in which each student interviews a friend about her or his favorite national holiday, time in class could be spent writing effective, open-ended interview questions before the students conduct their interviews. If the teacher plans to spend one class period writing interview questions, but finds that students struggle with composing open-ended questions, he or she may to need reteach the content in a different manner in the next class and provide students with additional time to draft the interview questions. Cooper and Murphy (2016) have articulated it best, noting that instructors must "reserve the right to mini lesson" (p. 98). Without the flexibility to reteach difficult concepts or skills, students' final projects may suffer. As facilitator of the project, the instructor must ensure that students are set up for success.

If the instructor notices multiple students struggling with a specific concept, she or he can create a mini lesson to use during a workshop day. Below is a mini lesson for the recipe project (see Chapter 2) designed to help students write a recipe for the class cookbook.

Objective: Students will be able to write a recipe using proper measurements.

Instructional Phase: The teacher reviews the measurements and models how to sequence a recipe using the proper measurements.

Guided Practice: As a class, students and the teacher write out a recipe for making a peanut butter and jelly sandwich and display it on the board.

Independent Practice: Using the board work as a reference or model, students resume their workshop time and continue to write their recipes for the class cookbook.

Mini lessons such as the above example give students the opportunity to not only refine their English skills but also make progress on their projects.

REFLECTIVE QUESTION

- How do you currently use mini lessons in your teaching?

- After reading Chapter 3 thus far, how might you revise or adapt your use of mini lessons?

- Why might these changes be necessary?

Using a Process to Create a Final Product

As indicated so far, mini lessons help scaffold to the final project. Therefore, it is also important for teachers to consider the process students must use to create their projects. As with teaching writing, the teacher must use a process approach to assist students in completing their projects. Fischer (2018) has stated that the process used to complete projects is pertinent for the creation of a good final product. He argued that teachers often focus too much on the final product (e.g., cookbook, diorama) and lose sight of the process that students need to go through in order to create the product. While there is very limited research on the process used in PBL, it seems that turning to the field of second language writing is a natural fit. For example, the writing process is recursive in nature, meaning it allows students to revise, reinvent, draft, copyedit, and so on in a fluid rather than linear process. The writing process also allows students the flexibility to create meaningful texts in a manner that suits their individual needs. Below are a series of steps students may take to complete a writing assignment. Because the writing process is not linear, students may return to and/or use these strategies in no particular order. It depends on their needs as writers and how they best write.

- brainstorming and setting goals
- studying or analyzing sample texts
- gathering and organizing sources and/or ideas
- drafting and revising with feedback from instructor and peers
- editing
- reflecting

When completing a project, students use a process similar to the writing process. For example, in the recipe unit, students were asked to brainstorm what recipes they would like to share with their classmates, they were asked to study models of recipes, they drafted and rehearsed, they received feedback from their peers and teachers, and at the end of the project, they reflected on the process they used to create the final product.

Facilitating the Process

As discussed earlier in this chapter, a teacher's role in PBL is to serve as a facilitator. Like a writing teacher, she or he guides students in a collaborative environment through the completion of the project. Because the process is recursive, teachers can use mini lessons to address concepts or content that students struggle with, or they may choose to individually confer with a student during class workshop time.

REFLECTIVE QUESTIONS

- How do you teach the writing process to your students?

- What activities or strategies do you use when taking your students through the process of creating a project or writing an essay?

Conclusion

This chapter discussed best practices for implementing PBL in the classroom, including designing and using mini lessons through a recursive process approach similar to the writing process in order for students to complete their projects. The next chapter discusses complete implementation of PBL in the classroom.

CHAPTER 4

Teaching PBL: Planning and Executing Lessons

This chapter presents a project used in an advanced-level course for adult English language learners. Formative and summative assessments are also included in the sample project so that audience members can use best teaching and assessment practices when using PBL. In addition, differentiated instruction is discussed.

By the end of this chapter, you will be able to answer the following question:

- What are best practices for implementing PBL in a classroom?

Project Background Information

The students who completed this project were adult English language learners in their last semester of an intensive English language program. They were all preparing to enter a graduate program of study. They completed the project in their advanced reading class, which emphasized reading professional journal articles. Each class period was 50 minutes. The class objectives call for students to be able to do the following:

- reflect on, analyze, and synthesize texts
- continue to outline or annotate advanced-level texts such as professional journal articles
- explain and analyze an author's purpose for writing and the intended audience
- distinguish between qualitative and quantitative research
- identify and analyze research questions presented in primary research studies
- locate, identify, and analyze archival texts

Day 1 (50-minute class period). The class objectives call for students to distinguish between qualitative and quantitative research and to reflect on, analyze, and synthesize texts. In order for the teacher to assess students' ability to meet these objectives, students read and annotate a professional journal article (in this example, "Language Challenges Faced by International Students in the United States" [Kuo, 2011]). After reading the article, students complete the activity outlined in Table 2.

Table 2. Activity Based on Article by Kuo (2011)

Write a citation for the article as it would appear in a reference page.

Who participated in the study?

Is the study qualitative or quantitative? How do you know?

What is the author's research question(s)?

What instruments (e.g., survey, interview) did the author use to conduct the study?

Did the author answer his or her research questions? Why or why not?

Write a one- to two-paragraph summary of the article.

Write one to two paragraphs critiquing the author's study. Was it well organized? Why or why not? Were there any flaws in the study design? How could the author improve?

Write one to two paragraphs reflecting on the study. How would this study help you in your future career? Could you replicate the study? If so, how?

Day 2. After students complete the assignment, they are placed into groups and assigned a project that requires them to use Kuo's (2011) findings to build their own primary research study and then present their findings in a multimodal composition. Table 3 shows the assignment sheet and rubric students receive.

Table 3. Assignment Sheet and Rubric

Primary Source Assignment Sheet
For any research assignment, primary research can be helpful, as it can be a supplement for secondary (library) research. For this assignment, you will interview a peer or survey a group of students about their studies in the United States based on the findings from Kuo's (2011) article. In other words, you will use Kuo's findings to help you write questions for the interview or survey. As a class, we will spend time writing good questions and preparing for the interviews and surveys. After you have completed your primary research, you will present your findings in a multimodal composition such as a video, Prezi, or PowerPoint. You may pick the platform, but you are expected to meet the following expectations. ● Your multimodal composition should have a clear introduction and conclusion. ● The composition should be well organized and take an outside audience into consideration. ● Your findings from the survey or interview should be clearly presented to your audience. ● You should clearly analyze your findings and put forth a plan for further research. ● Pictures, music, and other images and/sound effects should be connected to your topic. Below is the rubric that I will use to assess your final project.

continued on next page

Table 3. *(continued)*

Primary Research Rubric			
Criteria	**Developing**	**Acceptable**	**Excelling**
Introduction and conclusion	No thesis Conclusion does not summarize findings or reflect on research question	Indirect thesis Conclusion attempts to summarize and reflect on research question	Direct thesis with clear map for audience Conclusion contains a thorough summary of findings and thoughtful reflection
Development	No connection to Kuo's article No description of findings No analysis of findings	Attempts to connect to Kuo's article Some description of findings but could be further developed Some analysis of findings but could be further developed	Clear connection to Kuo's article Clear and cohesive description of findings Thoroughly developed analysis of findings
Organization and style	Headings are not used Images are not used Too much written text is used Audience is not considered	Headings are used Images are used but may not connect to findings or may be sparse and/or overused Text use is limited in most sections Audience is considered	Headings effectively highlight main points Images effectively refer to main points Text communicates with an audience throughout Audience's background knowledge and attitude about topic are considered
Documentation	Assignment is not composed in standard APA	Assignment is composed in APA but there may be small errors in text and/or the references page	APA is used correctly throughout the assignment

After the instructor introduces the assignment and review the assignment sheet and rubric, students return to the assignment completed on Day 1 and begin to brainstorm research questions that they would like to answer through their own primary research. Table 4 is a lesson plan for Day 2 of the unit.

Table 4. Lesson Plan for Day 2

Objective: Students will be able to write open-ended research questions.

Instructional phase: The teacher explains the difference between a yes/no and an open question, and then returns to Kuo's study and asks students to identify her research question and explain whether it is an open-ended question. The teacher then explains how to avoid writing biased research questions. She returns to Kuo's study and asks students to discuss whether the research questions were biased.

Guided practice: Together as a class, students and teacher write on the whiteboard practice research questions that are open-ended and avoid bias.

Independent practice: Using the notes on the whiteboard as a reference, students write a research question(s) for their studies.

Assessment of the objective: The teacher serves as a facilitator as students work in order to ensure each student has written an effective research question(s).

Day 3. After students write their research question(s), they consider whether they would use a survey or an interview to answer the question(s). Table 5 shows a lesson plan for Day 3.

Table 5. Lesson Plan for Day 3

Objective: Students will be able to define and identify the differences between qualitative and quantitative research. They will be able to construct an effective survey or interview depending on their individual research goals and research questions.

Instructional phase: The teacher reviews qualitative and quantitative research, and then has students discuss which type of research they plan to use for this assignment. The teacher then models how to effectively write survey and interview questions.

Guided practice: As a class and with teacher assistance, students write practice survey and/or interview questions.

Independent practice: Students individually draft their survey or interview questions and bring them to the next class period.

Assessment of the objectives: The teacher assess students based on their draft of survey or interview questions.

Day 4. The instructor conferences individually with each student to offer feedback on his or her survey or interview questions. At this point, some students are required to revise before they conduct their research. Once students have good questions, they are given permission to go ahead and begin conducting their research.

Day 5. Field day. Students use this class period to conduct their interviews or proctor surveys.

Day 6. Students bring their completed surveys and interviews to class and begin to identify themes or trends in their research. Table 6 shows a lesson plan for Day 6.

Table 6. Lesson Plan for Day 6

> **Objective:** Students will be able to identify themes in their primary research.
>
> Instructional phase: The teacher defines *theme* and asks students if they noticed any themes in their surveys. The teacher then models how to identify themes in primary research and use Kuo's article as a reference for students.
>
> **Guided practice:** In groups, students identify the themes Kuo noted in her article.
>
> Independent practice: Students individually analyze their survey or interview results and identify two to three themes.
>
> **Assessment of objective:** The teacher checks with each student to ensure he or she has identified at least three findings from the survey or interview results. This can be done in class during the independent practice phase, or it can be done during the next class period.

Days 7–9. Students take their findings and begin transforming them into a multimodal composition. As previously noted, students select which mode in which to present their findings. Students use these days to workshop their projects while the instructor individually conferences with students over their work to ensure they remain on task to complete the assignment.

Day 10. Students engage in a peer review session. The instructor places students into small groups and has them review each other's work and offer feedback for revising.

Days 11–12. Students present their multimodal compositions to the class. After they finish, they complete a written reflection in which they discuss the strengths of their projects, the weaknesses, and what they would do to improve if given more time.

Figure 1 shows a screenshot of a project. This group created a survey in which they asked international students to self-identify their academic language weaknesses and strengths. They presented their findings in a PowerPoint. In the slide in Figure 1, they provide a graph to show the participants' answers to a survey question. They then connected their finding to Kuo's (2011) article.

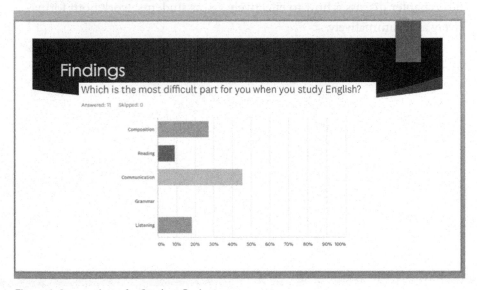

Figure 1. Screenshot of a Student Project

This project took 12 (50-minute) class periods to complete and offered students greater ability to meet the course objectives. It also further developed their higher order language and critical thinking skills. The process used to complete the project allowed the instructor to informally assess student learning to ensure they were on task to complete the project. Once students finished the project and reflected on their work, the instructor used the rubric to assess their final products.

Conclusion

This chapter presented a thorough look at how a teacher implemented PBL in a classroom from start to finish. As noted, PBL requires a large time commitment and requires the instructor to multitask, as students may experience different roadblocks and/or successes as they complete their projects. Indeed, differentiated instruction is so important with PBL. The next chapter discusses how to effectively assess students' work both formatively and summatively.

CHAPTER 5

Assessing PBL

This chapter explains how to use formative and summative assessments for PBL, including rubric design and use. In addition, reflection is discussed as a means for ongoing assessment throughout the completion of a project.

By the end of this chapter, you will be able to answer the following questions:

- How can a teacher use formative assessments to assess PBL?
- How can a teacher use summative assessments to assess PBL?
- Why is reflection important when assessing a project?

Unlike task-based instruction that relies on in-class work, homework, and perhaps quizzes and/or exams, PBL requires more extensive assessment. We can look at the assessment of projects through two lenses: formative and summative.

Formative Assessments

Formative assessments inform an instructor about a student's individual progress throughout the process of completing a project. Therefore, it is important for teachers to assess student learning throughout the project to determine "who gets it" (Cooper & Murphy, 2016, p. 107). Assessing students' daily progress means that there are fewer surprises when students turn in in their final projects because students should have already received feedback throughout the process of creating their projects.

For example, on the first day of the recipe project (see Chapter 1), the instructor introduces the assignment sheet and the rubric. Then, she or he explains and models the different measurements and the proper abbreviations used in recipes. In order to assess whether students recognize the measurements, and could use the measurements properly, the instructor has students complete an activity in class.

Rather than passively sit in the back of the classroom as students complete the task, the instructor observes students in their groups and offers them feedback and/or reteaches concepts to struggling students. The instructor pushes the excelling students and encourages them to do more by introducing advanced vocabulary to include in their projects, thereby informally ascertaining who met the objectives for the class period. If all students are on track, then the instructor can move to the next task.

On the second day, the teacher uses formative assessment to ensure students have effectively brainstormed. Indeed, good brainstorming informs students' final projects. If they picked a confusing or difficult recipe, with ingredients that are not readily available where they live, then it may be difficult for to complete the project. If they selected a dish with difficult words to pronounce, then they may struggle presenting in front of the class. It is important for the teacher to observe student learning and have conversations with students throughout the process, especially in the brainstorming stage, as this is the step where students are set up for success. Therefore, it is important for teachers to observe student learning throughout the process of completing the project.

Guidelines for Teachers Observing PBL Lessons

Chapman and King (2005) have put forth guidelines for teachers when they observe student learning in PBL:

- Recognize and use the student's prior knowledge (schema building).
- Identify individual learners' needs, including gaps in knowledge and/or application.
- Identify the students' "observable behaviors." (p. 29)

After taking into consideration students' prior knowledge, their individual needs, and behaviors, the instructor can best facilitate and assess student learning. As previously noted, because PBL allows for workshop days and individual conferencing, the instructor has time to further identify and address any gaps in students' language skills and proficiency through one-on-one moments of instruction.

REFLECTIVE QUESTION

- How can a teacher best informally assess student learning in PBL?

Summative Assessment

Clearly, formative assessment is important in ensuring students are on track to successfully complete their projects. Yet there comes a time when the instructor needs to step aside and stop facilitating; the process must come to an end. At this point, the teacher must assess students' final projects through a summative lens. Unlike formative assessment, which includes in-class assessments or homework assignments, summative assessment requires a more formal look at student learning. Summative assessment takes place at the end of a unit or project. And it is at this point that students receive grades and final feedback on their work.

For some projects, a rubric or checklist may be appropriate to assess student learning. For example, on the first day of the recipe unit, the instructor gives students an assignment sheet and rubric (see Table 7). The assignment sheet outlines the instructor's expectations for the project, and the rubric clearly articulates how students would be assessed on their projects.

Table 7. Assignment Sheet and Rubric for the Recipe Unit

Preparing and Sharing a Recipe
For this project, you will ● write a recipe (a dish of food from your home country); ● prepare the dish for your classmates, explaining how they can prepare the dish; ● with the help of your classmates, create a cookbook that includes a biography, at least two pictures of you and/or the food, and your recipe. We will spend time in class learning how to read and write recipes. Once you can read and write them, you will prepare the dish for your classmates. You will show and tell your classmates how to prepare your dish (just like a cooking show). After you have shown your classmates how to make your recipe, and we have all sampled the food, we will take all the recipes and create a class cookbook. In the cookbook, you will include pictures of the dish, the recipe, and a biography (a paragraph about yourself). I hope this will be a nice memory for you!

continued on next page

Project-Based Learning

Table 7. *(continued)*

	Developing	Acceptable	Excelling
Composition of recipe	Recipe is not composed using proper measurements	Recipe is composed using proper measurements	Recipe is composed using proper measurements and provides the audience with a clear understanding of how to make the recipe
Presentation of the dish	Student does not clearly explain how to prepare the recipe	Student clearly explains how to prepare the recipe	Student clearly explains how to prepare the recipe while engaging with the audience
	Student does not use props when presenting	Student uses props when presenting	Student uses props when presenting to engage the audience and further enhance their understanding of how to prepare the dish
Design and composition of the cookbook	Student's portion of the cookbook is not properly organized or developed	Student's portion of the cookbook is well organized and developed	Student' portion of the cookbook is well organized and developed and engages the audience
	The images do not match the written text	The images compliment the written text	The images compliment the written text and enhance the audience's understanding of the text
	There are more than 20 spelling, grammar, and/or punctuation errors in student's portion of the cookbook	There are 10–19 spelling, grammar, and/or punctuation errors in student's portion of the cookbook	There are fewer than 10 errors in student's portion of the cookbook

The rubric provides students with a guide to follow as they complete their projects. It also helps keep the instructor focused while grading, as she or he should assess only the areas noted on the rubric. If the instructor sees an issue or error in the student's work but it is not indicated on the rubric, and it was not addressed through class instruction, the instructor cannot "punish" the student for something that was not addressed beforehand. For example, if while grading the instructor finds that students did not use transitions in their biographies for the cookbook, but she or he never taught transitions and they are not indicated on the rubric, then the instructor cannot penalize students for the error. The instructor should simply make note to add transitions to the rubric and cover them the next time she or he teaches the unit.

While assessing the projects, the instructor may simply circle, highlight, check, and/or record notes on the rubric where the student falls. Table 8 is an example of a portion of the completed rubric for the recipe unit. Notice how the instructor highlights areas of the rubric and provides short comments in bold for the student. When the instructor returns the rubric to the student, the latter will see where she or he fell in regard to the work and receive written feedback on what she or he excelled in and could do improve. This type of feedback is necessary so the student can continue to hone her or his language skills.

Table 8. Partial Completed Rubric for the Recipe Project

	Developing	Acceptable	Excelling
Presentation of the dish	Student does not clearly explain how to prepare the recipe	Student clearly explains how to prepare the recipe	Student clearly explains how to prepare the recipe while engaging with the audience **Good eye contact. You explained your recipe well. I liked how you called on your classmates during the cooking demo. It kept your audience engaged.**
	Student does not use props when presenting	Student uses props when presenting **You were well prepared, but you forgot chopsticks! The rest of your props were good.**	Student uses props when presenting to engage the audience and further enhance their understanding of how to prepare the dish

REFLECTIVE QUESTION

- How do we actually know that our students read our feedback and use our comments to improve their English skills?

Assessment and Reflection

As noted in Chapter 2, reflection is an important piece of PBL, because it informs assessment of the project. Therefore, at the end of each project, students should reflect on some or all of the following points.

- how they contributed to the their groups
- how well the group collaborated (or didn't)
- the strengths of the project
- if given more time, how they would improve

Having students reflect on their projects helps inform how instructors assess student work. Unfortunately, there is little research on PBL and reflection practices in regard to assessment. However, as noted earlier, reflection is also important when teaching students how to compose. Thus, much of the research on reflection in PBL can be pinpointed to the field of second language writing and composition pedagogy. For example, Yancey (1998), in her groundbreaking text, has written,

In the language of assessment, students, by means of a reflection, are asked to locate their own work—measure what it purports to measure—precisely because it requires that students narrate, analyze, and evaluate their own learning their own texts and thus connect the assessment to their own learning. (p. 146)

Through reflection, student learning becomes more apparent to instructors and students. For example, Kammrad and Johnson (2017) have ELLs reflect on what they revise, delete, and add to their papers throughout the writing process. Instructors, who have students constantly reflect in this way, can turn to students' reflections when assessing work, especially for borderline students to determine whether they are making strong connections to their own learning.

Indeed, the ability to self-reflect is an extremely important metacognitive skill that increases students' ability to critically think, and it should be considered when grading a project. Cooper and Murphy (2016, p. 75) have recommended using "progress assessment tools" to encourage students to take ownership of their work. They have recommended that student set goals and reflect on the completion of these goals throughout the projects.

Checklists and graphic organizers can help students document their work on an ongoing basis. Table 9 is an example of a table adapted from Cooper and Murphy (2016) that students can use as they work on their projects. At the end of each class period, the instructor may ask students to quickly complete the table to reflect on what they have accomplished and what they would like to accomplish during the next class periods.

Table 9. Sample Graphic Organizer for Student Reflection

Day	What I (or the group) accomplished	Self-reflection	Goals for tomorrow
1			
2			
3			
4			
5			

REFLECTIVE QUESTIONS

- Think about how you use assignment sheets and rubrics in your own teaching. What currently works well for you?

- After reading this chapter, what might you change in regard to your formative and summative assessment practices?

- How might you use reflection to inform your assessment of student learning?

Conclusion

This chapter focused on best practices for effectively assessing projects. It also discussed how to use student reflection to ensure students stay on task and make the most of in-class workshop time. The next chapter discusses motivation as another means for keeping students engaged and on task when completing their projects.

CHAPTER 6

Possible Challenges

This chapter discusses best practices for keeping students engaged and on task when using PBL. It also offers instructors a means to avoid potential challenges or pitfalls when they embark on implementing PBL in their classrooms, such as how to motivate learners.

By the end of this chapter, you will be able to answer the following question:

- How can an instructor motivate students to fully participate in the process of completing a project?

We've all had times when we want to try something new in our classrooms. We spend countless days planning, creating materials, and the list goes on, and then things don't go the way we thought they would. Our students may not be invested. They may not be able to complete the project in the amount of time allotted. The materials designed may not be helpful.

- Reflect on a time when a lesson or project did not go the way you thought it would. What went wrong?

- How did you improve or revise for the next time you taught the lesson or project?

Some teachers may be hesitant to use PBL, because if something does go wrong, then it may seem like a waste of several weeks of class. Indeed, PBL can pose risks, but they are worth taking. And we can learn from past research about how to best prepare for PBL.

First off, some students may struggle to work in a more open learning environment. Beckett (2002) found some students are hesitant to embrace PBL, because they prefer a more traditional learning environment such as lecture-based instruction or learning from a textbook. For students who are more accustomed to teacher-centered learning, PBL—specifically collaboration with peers—can be difficult and does not happen automatically. It must be taught in a classroom setting so students can work on their projects in a safe environment.

Cooper and Murphy (2016) have advocated for teachers to model effective collaboration. Modeling also helps the more hesitant students recognize the value of collaboration. For students who are new to collaborative learning, it may be best to scaffold collaboration, beginning with modeling the act and then having students collaborate on smaller tasks in the classroom so the instructor can monitor their progress, before introducing a larger project. To model effective collaboration, an instructor can make use of role-play or, for more advanced learners, video record effective peer group sessions and have students analyze how they work in groups to accomplish or complete a task.

In addition, Beckett (2002) conducted a study about PBL in an intensive English program for adult learners and found that attendance dropped off in some English classrooms. Coming to class, especially for college-age ELLs, is a struggle. If they do not value a class or if they are uncomfortable, no doubt, they will not attend. It is thus the teacher's responsibility to show the value of PBL. This can be done through modeling and/or discussion. It might also behoove the teacher to assign homework or participation points for workshop days, peer review days, and/or conferences. This strategy might motivate learners to get out of bed to attend, work, and learn.

REFLECTIVE QUESTIONS

- How might an instructor model effective collaboration?

- Think about your students who are unmotivated. What strategies do you use to engage them and encourage them to complete work on time?

- Now think about the intrinsically motivated students. How do you ensure their work does not "suffer" because of their unmotivated peers?

Motivating Learners

As previously noted, PBL places a great deal of responsibility on students. Those who are unmotivated may not take as much interest in the projects; they may not work well with their peers; they may do minimal work outside of class. Indeed, teachers may need to think of other ways to motivate these students. Brown and Lee (2015) have noted that one way to motivate students is to give them choices in their work. Because PBL is flexible, instructors can design options for students. For example, in the recipe unit, students are allowed to select their own recipes for the cookbook. If it is a dish they love, perhaps a memory from home, the students may be more engaged in the project. In the primary research project, students are allowed to select the platform in which they present their research findings to an audience. Giving students these choices within the parameters of the project can motivate them to do their best work and collaborate with peers.

Table 10 shows a project for an advanced-level seminar class for ELLs. The culminating project for this course asks students to reflect on their experiences in the university. Students are given choices on what they reflect on and the mode in which they present their work. While they individually craft their project, they are given time to collaborate on peer review and workshop days.

Table 10. First-Year Seminar Final Project

Take some time to reflect on the semester. What did you learn? What did enjoy? What did you dislike? Was there a person or a group of people who helped you or who you enjoyed spending time with?

Create a multimodal composition in which you reflect on the semester. Your multimodal composition can be a poster, a PowerPoint, a Prezi, a video, or a podcast.

This project is considered your final exam. Therefore, you will present your work during the scheduled exam time to the class. Presentations/multimodal compositions should be no more than 5 minutes long.

Below is the schedule for completion of the project.

Monday (today)	Introduce project & begin brainstorming
Wednesday	Share brainstorming & analyze models of past multimodal projects
Friday	Workshop day
Monday	Peer review (bring a draft of your multimodal text)
Wednesday	Looking at the finer points of your project (e.g., grammar)
Friday	Rehearsal day
Monday	Present projects
Wednesday	Reflections due via e-mail (reflect on your multimodal composition and presentation)

Rubric			
	Developing	**Acceptable**	**Excelling**
Thesis and development	Project lacks a main point(s) and development is weak or off topic	Project contains a main point(s) but it may not be fully developed	Project contains a main point(s) that is fully developed and supported
Organization and style	Few if any transitions are used	Some use of single-word transitions throughout the project	Use of phrasal and sentence transitions to advance from point to point
	Project lacks audience awareness in some areas	Project is prepared for an appropriate audience	Project is prepared for an appropriate audience and considers the audience's background knowledge and attitude toward the topic
Mechanics, usage, grammar, spelling	Project contains more than 11 grammatical, spelling, or mechanical errors	Project contains 6–10 grammatical, spelling, or mechanical errors	Project contains 0–5 grammatical, spelling, or mechanical errors

As previously noted, students are given choices in the design and completion of this project. It is important to note that the instructor uses the same rubric to assess the different types of multimodal projects; there is no need to create separate rubrics for each type of multimodal assignment. Like with a research paper, students are assessed on their abilities to clearly articulate, support, and develop a thesis statement. They are also assessed on their ability to use effective transitions to move from one point to the next and compose for a specific audience. The ability to compose using these rhetorical conventions could be demonstrated in multiple modes such as a video, a Prezi, or even a web page. (For more on multimodal compositions and digital literacies, see Bloch & Wilkinson, 2014.)

Final Suggestions for Implementing PBL

Be realistic. While projects are a lot of time and work for the instructor, not everyone will perform within the excelling range of your rubric. And that's OK. It is also important to be realistic regarding our limitations as educators. We may not have access to the appropriate technology, we may be limited on time, or we may have students who do not work well on extended projects. As teachers, we need to keep these limitations in mind whenever we lesson plan, especially when we plan for PBL.

Accept that mistakes will happen. You may find mistakes in your assignment sheet and/or rubric. Be sure to note these errors and correct them for the next time. If you have failed to consider something in your lesson planning, make a note and fix it for the next time you assign the project. We take students through a process to complete their projects. We need to use a similar process as we create projects and lesson plans. There is always room for improvement and revision in our teaching.

Watch out for delays. As previously noted, you may need to tweak your daily lessons to accommodate struggling or excelling learners. It's a balancing act, but individualized instruction is very important with PBL.

Conclusion

This chapter provided additional advice for using PBL. Hopefully, instructors feel confident using PBL in their English language classrooms and find PBL to be an exciting option for students.

The purpose of this book was to provide a snapshot of best practices for designing, implementing, and assessing PBL in English language classrooms. Instructors who want to challenge their students and like to create a collaborative environment will no doubt find PBL an invigorating way to engage their students.

After reading this book, teachers are now ready to design, implement, oversee, and assess projects with ease and confidence. No doubt they will find PBL to be an enriching experience in which students improve their language and critical thinking skills.

References

Anderson, L., & Krathwohl, D. (2001). *A taxonomy for learning, teaching, and assessing.* New York, NY: Longman.

Beckett, G. (2002). Teacher and student evaluations of project-based learning. *TESL Canada Journal, 19*(2), 52–66.

Bloch, J., & Wilkinson, M. (2014). *Teaching digital literacies.* Alexandria, VA: TESOL International Association.

Brown, D., & Lee, H. (2015). *Teaching by principles.* New York, NY: Pearson.

Bygate, M., Skehan, P., & Swain, M. (Eds.). (2001). *Researching pedagogic tasks: Second language learning, teaching, and testing.* London, England: Longman.

Campbell, S. A. (2012). The phenomological study of ESL students in a project-based learning environment. *International Journal of Interdisciplinary Social Sciences, 6*(11), 139–152.

Chapman, C., & King, R. (2005). *Differentiated assessment strategies.* Thousand Oaks, CA: Corwin.

Cooper, R., & Murphy, E. (2016). *Hacking project based learning.* Cleveland, OH: Times 10.

Ellis, R. (2003). *The study of second language acquisition.* New York, NY: Oxford University Press.

Fischer, C. (2018). Project-based learning. Retrieved from http://connection.ebscohost.com/c/essays/28544207/project-based-learning

Hedge, T. (1993). Key concepts in ELT. *ELT Journal, 47,* 275–277.

Kammrad, L., & Johnson, C. (2017). Teaching to the big ideas of science. In B. Hand, L. Norton-Meier, & J. Jang (Eds.), *More voices from the classroom* (pp. 143–154). Boston, MA: Sense.

Kuo, Y. (2011). Language challenges faced by international graduate students in the United States. *Journal of International Students, 1*(2), 38–42.

Leat, D. (2017). *Enquiry and project based learning.* New York, NY: Routledge.

Lessard-Clouston, M. (2016). *Second language acquisition applied to English language teaching.* Alexandria, VA: TESOL International Association.

Long, M., & Porter, P. (1985). Group work, interlanguage talk, and second language acquisition. *TESOL Quarterly, 19,* 207–228.

Yancey, K. (1998). *Reflection in the writing classroom.* Logan: Utah State University Press.